THE SACRED PHALLUS

MAGICAL SYMBOL OF POWER AND PROTECTION

I0458631

GREGORY LEE WHITE

White Willow Press
Nashville, TN

The Sacred Phallus
Magical Symbol of Power and Protection
by
Gregory Lee White

Text:
Gregory Lee White

Cover Art:
Gregory Lee White
both the serpent and the athame are considered to be magical phallic symbols

Interior Illustrations:
artistic drawings and renderings of ancient artifacts

First Edition 2025

Published by
White Willow Press
211 Donelson Pike, Suite 111
Nashville, Tn 37214

Printed in the United States

ISBN: 978-1-965586-07-5

TABLE OF CONTENTS

OTHER BOOKS BY GREGORY LEE WHITE

Clucked – The Tale of Pickin Chicken

Making Soap from Scratch: How to Make Handmade Soap – A Beginners Guide and Beyond

Essential Oils and Aromatherapy - How to Use Essential Oils for Beauty, Health, and Spirituality

Little House Search – A Puzzle Book and Tour of the Works of Laura Ingalls Wilder

The Use of Magical Oils in Hoodoo, Prayer, and Spellwork

Papa Gee's Hoodoo Herbal - The Magic of Herbs, Roots, and Minerals in the Hoodoo Tradition

The Stranger in the Cup – How to Read Your Luck and Fate in the Tea Leaves by Gregory Lee White and Catherine Yronwode

How to Use Amulets, Charms, and Talismans in the Hoodoo and Conjure Tradition by Catherine Yronwode and Gregory Lee White

Lenormand Basics – How to Read Lenormand Cards for Beginners

Casting Love Spells – Rituals of Romance, Passion, and Attraction

Hex Appeal – How to Cast Dark Spells of Revenge, Cursing, and Damnation

Fairy Lore and Myths

Papa Gee's Book of Candle Magic

Cernunnos – The Lord of Wild Things

Hecate – The Goddess of Witchcraft

Tarot Magic: Spells, Spreads, and Sorcery Using the Tarot Deck

INTRODUCTION

The phallus has always been more than just a body part. Across the world, and throughout history, people have seen it as a powerful symbol—one that speaks of life, magic, strength, and spirit. It shows up in carvings, in temple walls, in old stories, and in sacred rituals. You'll find it on amulets, painted in alleyways, carried in processions, or tucked into the pocket of someone hoping for luck or fertility. This symbol has been with us a long time, and it's not going anywhere.

Some folks today might feel uncomfortable talking about it. But in the old ways, there was no shame in honoring the body—especially the parts that create life. Studying the phallus isn't about being vulgar. It's about understanding why so many different cultures used it in magic, in art, and in prayer. This book will help you understand why it mattered then and why it still matters now.

We're going to look at phallic symbols from every corner of the globe. From the tombs of Egypt to the temples of Thailand. From the Roman streets to the altars of hoodoo rootworkers. We'll follow the trail through myth, ritual, history, and magic. We'll even look at how it shows up in modern psychology and spiritual practice.

!

DEDICATION

To whoever first looked at one and said,
"I think there's magic in that."

You were absolutely right.

ACKNOWLEDGEMENTS

A bow and thank you to the author, Hargrave Jennings, who wrote the book *Phallic Worship* in 1880. You gave me the idea to bring this topic into the modern world and showcase its magic. His work was invaluable to the research behind this book.

THE PHALLIC SYMBOL IN ANCIENT CIVILIZATIONS

Before we ever carved temples or built towers, we carved something far more primal into stone: the phallus.

Now, I know what you're thinking. But this isn't about sex—not really. Not just. It's about energy. Life force. The wild spark that pushes the seed through soil and the storm across the sky. The phallus has always meant more than anatomy. In ancient magic, it stood as a living symbol—creation and protection, all wrapped into one sacred shape.

Long before written language, long before gods had names, our ancestors etched phallic images onto cave walls and sacred stones. These weren't graffiti or dirty jokes. They were prayers. Spells. Rituals of survival and fertility. The shape of the phallus wasn't a joke to them—it was a key. A map. A lightning rod for the divine. In places like Mesopotamia and Sumeria, the phallus was tied to gods of crops and storms. You honored the rod, and the rains came. You carved it into your tools, and the harvest grew tall. The god Dumuzid wasn't just a name—they believed he was the seed, the moisture, the thing that brought life from barren dirt. The stalk that stood upright when all else withered.

It wasn't just for farmers. Warriors, kings, and medicine men all turned to the phallus as a mark of spiritual might. You might find one carved into a weapon handle or hung around the neck of a tribal chief. You might even see one buried at the edge of a field like a talisman—marking that land as fertile, blessed, and protected. In some burial sites, phallic carvings were laid with the dead, meant to ensure virility in the afterlife, or to light the path of rebirth. To die with it was to be born again.

In Greece, they didn't whisper about it. They celebrated it. Publicly. Loudly. And with wine.

During festivals to Dionysus—the god of wine, madness, and divine ecstasy—entire towns carried massive wooden phalluses through the streets. Picture it: singing, dancing, offerings poured on the earth. These weren't polite ceremonies. These were rowdy invocations. The wild laughter was a spell. The procession itself was a form of prayer. They weren't trying to shock; they were honoring a force of nature. The phallus wasn't crude. It was divine. It connected humans to the gods, to joy, and to the raw energy of life.

These weren't metaphorical celebrations either. They were magical rites. When a town honored Dionysus with a procession of phallic symbols, they were calling on sacred protection. Asking for abundance. For ecstasy. For wild joy to bless the land. They believed laughter itself disoriented evil spirits. That joy was armor. That a visible, honored phallus was a guardian against envy and death.

Across smaller tribal cultures—far from temples and empires—you still found phallic charms tucked into daily life. A carved wooden phallus might hang above a family's door to protect against evil spirits. Warriors might paint one onto their shields before battle. A hunter might carry one as a charm of strength and virility. To them, this wasn't superstition. It was sacred practice. In parts of Mongolia and Siberia, shamans carried staffs topped with phallic heads—not as jokes, but as tools of spirit contact, fertility invocation, and protection from possession.

In Africa, South America, and the Pacific Islands, you'll still find the phallus honored in ceremony. In some places, tall poles are raised like antennas between earth and sky. In others, small charms are hidden in homes to bring luck, children, or strength. These sacred objects are often carved with care, blessed with prayer, and kept close to the body. You don't laugh at a lightning rod. You respect it. The phallus is no different.

Even today, in parts of rural India, you'll see stone lingams dedicated to the god Shiva—phallic in form, cosmic in meaning. These aren't idols. They're portals. Symbols of the universe's endless cycle: birth, death, rebirth. The lingam isn't worshipped because of what it looks like—it's honored because of what it does. It channels the creative spark. It holds cosmic direction. And it reminds us that the body is not separate from the divine. It's part of it.

Among the Celts, tree-trunks were stripped, carved, and planted upright in sacred groves—blessed by druids, honored in fire rituals, and danced around in springtime rites. Some scholars argue these were the ancestors of maypoles—phallic symbols wrapped in ribbon, crowned in flowers, celebrated by entire villages in seasonal festivals of fertility and joy.

In Japan, fertility shrines still house sacred phalluses carved from stone, polished by centuries of prayer and touch. Some are paraded annually through villages, covered in offerings, honored with music and dance. They're not hidden. They're lifted. And they bless everyone they pass.

So let's be clear. When we talk about the phallus in ancient civilization, we are not talking about vulgarity or obscenity. We're talking about sacred technology. Symbols that channeled power. Represented protection. Gave people hope, direction, and strength. The phallus was a magical tool. A divine key. A signpost for those walking between worlds.

And for those of us still practicing today, it still is. We don't need to invent a new language to honor life-force—we just need to remember the one our ancestors already carved in stone. The rod was never just flesh. It was will. It was blessing. It was the upright flame in a world that didn't always know where to turn.

And in our circles, our altars, our spellwork—it still stands.

EGYPTIAN WORSHIP

Down in the sands of Egypt, where gods walked beside men and the Nile flowed like a living serpent, symbols held more power than speech. In that ancient world, the phallus wasn't crude. It was sacred. It was carved into stone not to shock, but to honor the raw force of creation. It stood as a sign—not just of manhood, but of divine spark, resurrection, and cosmic will.

The Egyptians didn't separate magic from daily life. Everything was spiritual. They called it *heka*—not superstition, but a real power, a force that shaped the world like a potter shapes clay. The phallus played a central role in this. It was more than a body part. It was a vessel for the sacred.

Look to the story of Osiris if you want to understand how deep this went. Osiris, the god of the dead and the reborn, was torn to pieces by his jealous brother Set. Every part of him was scattered across the land. His wife, the goddess Isis, searched high and low, gathering his remains. But one part was missing—his phallus, swallowed by a fish in the Nile.

That could have been the end. But Isis was no ordinary wife—she was a sorceress. She made him whole again with her magic. She shaped a new phallus from gold or clay, depending on the version, and breathed divine breath into it. From that sacred act, she conceived Horus, the falcon-headed avenger who would reclaim Egypt and restore balance. That golden phallus wasn't metaphor—it was magic in its purest form: life brought forth from death, order restored from chaos.

This myth wasn't whispered behind closed doors. It was carved on temple walls, enacted in holy rites, and honored in the planting season. When priests reenacted the story of Osiris each year, they weren't just telling a tale—they were calling the crops to rise, asking the river to swell, and urging the land back to life. The phallus wasn't shameful. It was holy. It was the staff that brought the world back from the edge.

And it didn't end with Osiris.

Another god, Min, stood tall with an erect phallus in nearly every depiction. He was the god of fertility, crops, and masculine potency. His image is bold—he stands straight, one arm raised in blessing, the other grasping his manhood. Offerings of lettuce—an aphrodisiac to the Egyptians—were left at his feet. People prayed to him for children, livestock, and healthy harvests. They weren't asking for sex. They were asking for life, for strength, for endurance. And Min, firm and unflinching, promised to deliver.

Min's cult centers were sites of wild reverence. His festivals, like the *Coming Forth of Min*, included ritual processions, sacred dances, and sometimes even symbolic climbing of tall poles to represent his divine virility. The phallus, in Min's rites, was not hidden—it was raised, celebrated, and crowned. And when a new pharaoh was crowned, he often participated in fertility rituals honoring Min, affirming not just his political power, but his spiritual potency—the ability to bring order, growth, and legacy to the land.

To modern eyes, Min's statues may look shocking. But to the Egyptians, they were divine. Fertility was never hidden. It was celebrated. Obelisks—those tall, tapering pillars pointing to the heavens—were more than just architectural feats. They echoed the upright phallus. Firm. Reaching. Full of power. They called down light from Ra, the sun god, and rooted it in stone.

And those obelisks weren't just symbols. They were spiritual antennas—connecting heaven and earth, sun and soil, will and form. Priests believed they could anchor divine energy in place. Every carved inscription wasn't just a record—it was a spell, keeping that upright force humming with power for eternity.

Phallic energy also wove its way into the teachings of Hermeticism, the mystical philosophy that bridged Egypt and Greece. In these texts, creation was a union of opposites—masculine and feminine, spirit and flesh. The phallus, representing projection and will, symbolized divine force entering the world to set creation in motion. It was the spark striking the dark.

The wand pressing into the unknown. The "word" that becomes "flesh."

This symbolism didn't stay locked in Egyptian temples. It spread through Greece, then into Rome, and later into Western occult traditions. The magician's wand. The upright pillar on the altar. The rod of kings. All owe a debt to Egypt, where the phallus wasn't hidden but crowned.

Even everyday Egyptians wore phallic charms for protection—especially children and pregnant women. These amulets, often shaped like small erect phalluses, were believed to guard against evil and strengthen the life force. Some were carved from clay or stone. Others were painted in vibrant colors or forged from gold. They were carried through life and even into death—tucked into tombs to light the way to the afterlife.

One especially curious object found in tombs is the "captive phallus" or "phallic cage"—a charm or piece of jewelry that encased the phallus in a frame or net. Scholars debate its use. Was it protection? Control? A binding spell to focus energy inward? Whatever its meaning, the message is clear: sometimes, power must be contained to be most effective. The cage wasn't a denial of energy—it was its sacred vessel.

And let's not forget: Egyptian religion didn't draw hard lines between male and female when it came to sacred power. Gods could be androgynous.

Goddesses could wield masculine traits. Isis herself was sometimes called "the one who is male and female." That alone tells us something vital: the phallus, as a magical force, doesn't belong to one gender. It belongs to anyone who honors its meaning—will, strength, growth, and direction.

The tombs of the Valley of the Kings bear witness. Phallic imagery was carefully painted into tomb walls, woven into spells from the *Book of the Dead*, and even referenced in resurrection texts where the deceased was said to regain all their bodily parts—including the phallus—before entering the next life. No one could rise without it. No soul could ascend without its force restored.

From the Old Kingdom to the Greco-Roman era, the sacred phallus remained a cornerstone of Egyptian magic. It may have changed names or shapes, but its power never waned. It was a symbol of rebirth, divine will, and cosmic fertility. It stood tall in rituals, lived in amulets, and echoed through architecture. You could see it in the way a temple was shaped, in the staff a priest carried, even in the language they used—words rising with force, like spells struck with the rod.

For today's practitioner, there's still wisdom to draw from these sands.

Don't separate spirit from body. Don't mock what once was holy. Symbols carry the weight we give them—and when they are fed with reverence, story, and faith, they grow. The golden phallus of Osiris. The unwavering presence of Min. The humble amulet wrapped in cloth. These are not just relics. They are lessons. They are tools. And they still work.

A collection of Roman facinus, 2nd century AD

THE PALAD KHIK

There's a small object you'll find all over Thailand—dangling from keychains, hanging above altars, or carved into the wood of roadside stalls. At first glance, it might make a Westerner blush. It's a penis. Plain as day. But this isn't just decoration or novelty. It's a Palad Khik—a sacred, carved phallus used in Thai magic for protection, prosperity, and power.

The name *Palad Khik* roughly means "honorable surrogate penis." Now let that settle in. This isn't crude. It's reverent. It carries centuries of spiritual practice carved into its wooden or metal form. You see, what some may laugh at, others pray with. And those who understand its roots don't laugh at all.

These charms are blessed—often by monks or spirit doctors known as *arjan*—and inscribed with powerful symbols. Ancient Khmer or Pali script is etched deep into their surface, not for decoration but for activation. Every line, every swirl, every deity face added to the charm is a spell. An invocation. A contract between spirit and flesh.

The Palad Khik is a worker. It draws in what is good—money, love, favor—and pushes out what is not. Curses, bad spirits, accidents, and misfortune are deflected. It doesn't matter if you're a merchant in Bangkok or a taxi driver cruising through Chiang Mai—many keep one in their glovebox or tuck it into their belt, trusting in the power of the charm to keep them safe and thriving. In fact, it's so common that local regulations in some areas of Thailand quietly advise against wearing them into government offices—not out of disrespect, but because their presence demands reverence, not bureaucracy.

But this phallic protector didn't originate in Thailand. Its deeper history lies in the roots of Hinduism—in the worship of Shiva, the god of creation and destruction. The *lingam*, Shiva's sacred symbol, is not just a representation of the phallus; it is a cosmic emblem. It stands for divine will, the axis of the universe, the living pulse of creation. And over time, as Buddhism traveled from India through Southeast Asia, that sacred symbol was adapted, reinterpreted, and reborn as the Palad Khik.

This process, known as religious syncretism, allowed old gods to wear new names while retaining their power. The result? A talisman that blends folk magic with temple wisdom, soaked in oil and chant, then carved into form by hands that understand the divine. The Palad Khik carries both the roar of the spirit world and the whisper of the monk. It's rural protection and high ritual, all carved into one small, potent shape.

Now, don't think these are all one shape or size. Some are tiny—small enough to wear discreetly around the neck. Others are bold and ceremonial, adorned with tusks, fangs, or animals of power like tigers and *nagas*. Some laugh. Some threaten. Some show expressions of bliss. All of them speak a magical language older than most written alphabets.

When a Palad Khik is made properly, it is not simply carved—it is awakened.

The blessing of the charm often includes ritual chanting called *katha*, along with sacred oil, incense, and breath. The monk or spiritual teacher does not simply say a prayer. They breathe life into it. That moment is when the charm becomes more than art. It becomes alive in the magical sense. It becomes a guardian, a carrier of intention, a shield woven from wood and word.

Some even say these charms can save lives.

One story tells of a man who kept his Palad Khik tucked into his waistband. When attacked by a knife-wielding assailant, the blade struck the charm instead—and bounced off. In another tale, a business escaped destruction during a city fire, while every other shop on the block burned. Only the one with a blessed Palad Khik hanging above the entrance remained untouched. Coincidence? The old spirits would say otherwise.

The phallus, in this form, becomes a guardian. A wall against harm. A bridge between intention and result. Just like the scarecrow-like statues of Priapus in ancient Rome, or the household obelisks in Egypt, the Palad Khik is often placed at thresholds—doorways, gates, shop entrances. It says to unseen forces: "Stop here. If you mean harm, you may not pass."

That threshold magic runs deep in every culture. A door is not just wood and hinges. It's a crossing point between worlds. The Palad Khik is a sentinel standing watch.

But here's something most folks miss: the Palad Khik is not just about sex or virility. It's about *life-force*.

In magical terms, we call this energy *vitality*—that spark that makes crops grow, that drives wind across oceans, that urges the body to rise and move forward. The Palad Khik holds that energy in concentrated form. You don't need to be male to benefit from it. This is not about gender—it's about power. Protection. Momentum. The will to survive and thrive.

And while most wearers are men, plenty of women also use these charms—for business success, fertility, safety, or to ward off spiritual harm. In this way, the charm becomes less about the body it resembles and more about the power it channels. The Palad Khik doesn't care who you are. It responds to how you use it.

Some even claim that the Palad Khik can grant invisibility—not literal, but spiritual. It confuses hostile spirits, distracts malicious energies, and makes the wearer less visible to danger. It's a magical cloak stitched in symbolism and belief. The phallus, in this form, doesn't seduce—it defends.

In rural villages, it's not uncommon to see them tucked into the eaves of homes, hanging above cash registers, or nailed to wooden posts where two roads meet. This isn't superstition—it's folk technology. The same way a scarecrow isn't just decoration. It's functional. It's charged with purpose. And the spirits know the difference.

Now, in the West, folks might scoff. A wooden penis on a keychain? Surely that's a joke, they say.

But magic doesn't need your permission to work. It only needs your belief. And in Thailand, belief runs deep.

The spirits know what the symbol means. The ancestors recognize the shape. The gods remember the rituals. When you carry a Palad Khik, you're not holding a novelty. You're holding centuries of faith, carved into form and still breathing. And if you ask those who carry one why it works, they won't hand you a theology book. They'll tell you what they know: that luck came when it was needed, that harm missed its mark, and that protection held firm when the winds blew sharp. That's not theory. That's memory.

So let others laugh. Let tourists take pictures and roll

their eyes. But those who understand—the merchants, the monks, the grandmothers who anoint the charm with whispered prayers—know better. They know the Palad Khik is not an ornament. It is a ward. A will. A woven link between body and spirit, between the earthly and the divine. And in a world full of noise and distraction, to carry something that has power—real, tested, ancestral power—is no small thing.

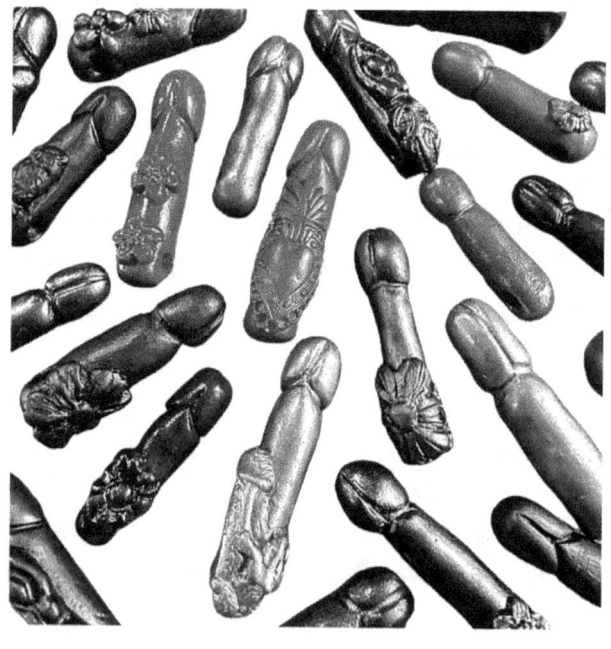

A collection of Palad Khik amulets sculpted by the author out of polymer clay.

THE ROMAN FACINUS

To understand the place the phallus held in Roman life, you don't need to search dusty temples or scrolls. Just walk the ruins of Pompeii. Look closely. You'll find it everywhere—sculpted above doorways, painted on tavern walls, even set into sidewalks. Pointing. Smiling. Swinging in the breeze from garden statues. The erect phallus in Rome was no secret. It was no shame. It was sacred protection.

At the heart of this protection stood *Fascinus*—not just a symbol, but a spirit. A living embodiment of divine phallic energy.

Now, that name may sound familiar. It gave us the word *fascinate*, and rightfully so. *Fascinus* had the power to charm, bewitch, and repel evil—especially that insidious force the Romans feared most: the evil eye. Jealousy. Ill will. The look that kills crops, curses children, or spoils a soldier's luck in battle. And what better to repel that kind of darkness than a bold, winged, laughing penis?

That's right. The Romans didn't whisper about protection—they put it on display.

Small charms called *fascina* were worn by everyone from commoners to emperors. Children wore them to ward off harm. Soldiers carried them into war. Even the high priest of the Vestal Virgins—Rome's holiest women—would suspend a *Fascinus* amulet beneath their sacred chariot. Think about that. The guardians of Rome's purity riding under a charm shaped like an erect penis. That should tell you this wasn't crude. This was holy magic.

Rome treated magical protection as a public concern. It wasn't hidden in back rooms or cloaked in secrecy. It was hammered into metal, strung on cords, and nailed to gates. You could find *fascina* swinging from the necks of infants, carved into the prows of ships, or embedded in home altars. These weren't decorations—they were spiritual tools. Activated through intention and worn like armor.

Romans also loved their *tintinnabula*—wind chimes fashioned from bronze, shaped like winged phalluses, often with animal limbs and fierce little faces. These hung in doorways and gardens. When the wind blew, they clattered, jingled, and cackled like a chorus of tiny tricksters. Their message? "Back off, evil. You're not welcome here."

And that wasn't just metaphor. Romans believed in *numen*—a sacred force that pulsed through every living thing, every river, every object. And the phallus, being the source of creation, was bursting with it. It was a vessel of *numen*. A walking, dancing, hanging spiritual battery. When cast in bronze and blessed, it became a kind of magical engine. Constant. Protective. Unapologetic.

Then there was Priapus.

Born of Aphrodite and Dionysus—or sometimes Hermes or Pan—Priapus was cursed by Hera. His fate? An enormous, eternal erection... but no ability to consummate. Banished from Olympus, he took root among fields and farms, becoming a god of gardens, livestock, and boundaries.

His statues stood at the edges of land and home—naked, bold, and unmistakable. And often, they came with warnings.

"Beware," one might say, "lest Priapus find you bending over."

It was a joke. But it was also a spell.

Humor was part of Roman magic. Laughter confused the spirits, scattered ill intent, and let divine power slip in through the cracks. A charm that made you laugh also made you safe. The ridiculous wasn't weakness—it was ward. It unseated fear. And if spirits got too close, the shock of the image sent them scurrying. The Romans understood that sometimes the best protection wasn't solemn—it was bold. Loud. Even absurd.

Priapus wasn't just for scaring off thieves and spirits. Farmers left offerings to him for fertile crops. Travelers prayed to him at boundaries. Lovers honored him with songs and carved phalluses placed in vineyards and orchards. His statues often included inscriptions—part threat, part blessing. His role was guardian and giver. He didn't just watch over the land. He fed it.

And like all good magic, the phallic protections of Rome were living tools. They were activated by belief and placed with intention. Hung by beds to inspire fertility. Carried into dice games for luck. Worn as necklaces to keep spirits at bay. This wasn't superstition—it was sacred survival. It was practical spellwork in public life.

Rome, as always, absorbed from others. The phallic worship of Greece—Pan and Dionysus, with their wine-fueled fertility—merged easily into Roman myth. The gods were renamed, the festivals rebranded, but the energy remained the same. Erect. Magical. Alive.

And while many of the charms were worn by men, women also participated fully in this tradition. During the festival of Liberalia, Roman women paraded through the streets with phallic effigies, sometimes crowned in flowers. These weren't drunken parties. They were rituals of life and rebirth. Honoring Liber, a god of seeds, growth, and freedom—both in the soil and the soul.

Liber formed part of the Aventine Triad alongside Ceres and Libera—gods of agriculture, fertility, and the working class. Their temple stood tall on the Aventine Hill, and their rites were filled with music, laughter, and ecstatic joy. During the festival, boys would shed their childhood amulet, the *bulla*, and dedicate it to the gods. This public display of phallic symbols wasn't crude—it was initiation. A rite of passage. A magical act of becoming.

And it wasn't just spiritual.

Phallic charms were part of Roman medicine. Doctors might place a *fascinus* near a sick child's bed.

A healer might recommend one for protection after childbirth. Because the Romans believed what many of us forget today: the body and the spirit are not separate. Heal one, and you heal the other. The phallus, as a symbol of life-force, was a natural cure.

Some were made of bronze. Others were carved in stone or bone. Some were simple. Some were wild. But all of them were intentional. They were placed where energy crossed—thresholds, bedsides, cradles, and fields. They were defenders. Blessers. Joy-bringers. And they did their work boldly.

Even in battle, Roman soldiers carried phallic charms for protection—not just physical, but metaphysical. They believed that the phallus could shield them from curses laid by enemy priests, or the ill-wishing eyes of rival commanders. The upright form represented more than virility—it represented divine favor. The will to stand when others fell. And in the chaos of war, a little divine will was worth its weight in bronze.

So, while modern folks might smirk at the winged penis of Rome, the old world knew better.

The phallus wasn't obscene. It was divine. It carried laughter and thunder in equal measure. It was carved, worn, blessed, and raised—not for shock value, but for spiritual protection, social identity, and sacred power. It reminded the living that life begins with force, survives through direction, and thrives when spirit walks with flesh. In the Roman world, the phallus was not an object of ridicule—it was a god, a guardian, and a guide.

THE PHALLUS IN EASTERN TRADITIONS

Across India, Southeast Asia, the Himalayan highlands, and the islands of Japan, the phallus still stands—visible, honored, and worked with. Not as spectacle, but as sacred function. In these places, the symbol was never buried under shame. It remained what it had always been: a tool of power, a conduit of life, and a point of contact between the earthly and the divine.

Start with India, where the upright form of Shiva's *lingam* still receives thousands of offerings a day. Found in temples, riverbanks, roadside shrines, and family altars, the *lingam* is not just sculpture—it's a center of energy. It's the axis of creation. It rests in the *yoni*, the sacred feminine base, representing divine union, not sex. Will and form. Penetration and reception. Cosmic polarity in harmony.

The worship of Shiva through the *lingam* isn't ancient history—it's ongoing. During the holy month of *Shravan*, devotees carry water from sacred rivers to pour over *lingams*, chanting prayers for fertility, health, and purification. This is not metaphorical cleansing. It's active invocation. A way to rebalance what has stalled in one's body, household, or destiny. And in places like Kashi and Kedarnath, some *lingams* are said to have emerged on their own—*svayambhu*—not placed by humans, but risen by spirit. Those sites are considered especially potent.

In tantric traditions, the *lingam* becomes a vessel of focused will. Tantric initiates learn to channel energy through breath, mantra, and visualization, activating the *lingam* not as symbol but as force. In this context, the phallus is a spiritual engine, representing conscious direction. It's not about physical sex—it's about energetic command. Practitioners of all genders engage with this energy. It isn't owned. It's worked.

The shape of the phallus appears again in South Indian village festivals, where terracotta fertility icons called *lingams*, *naga stones*, or *kambam* are offered to the land to ensure rainfall and crop growth. These rites connect survival to direction. If the land is dry, something is blocked. The phallus, in these cases, becomes a ritual tool to restore flow. You don't theorize about it. You plant it in the field.

Keep moving east, and you reach Cambodia, where the temples of Angkor still bear the marks of divine union. Many *linga-yoni* altars remain intact, carved from sandstone and aligned with ancient water channels. In some ruins, small *lingams* sit half-buried, yet still honored with incense and flowers by locals who've never stopped believing in their presence. You'll find small offerings tucked into the moss— tokens of respect for a force that still answers when called.

In Bali, the phallus appears less formally but with the

same energy. Local forms of Hinduism blend with animism, and rituals for prosperity often involve planting upright sticks or stone markers at the edges of fields and homes. These phallic forms aren't always recognized as such by outsiders, but their meaning is clear to the people: strength, protection, and presence. A force that stands between your home and what threatens it.

Then there's Thailand, where the *Palad Khik* continues to bridge folk belief and monastic blessing. These carved charms are everywhere—in pockets, cars, shops, homes. They're blessed by monks in long rituals involving sacred incantation (*katha*), incense, and breath. Some are inscribed with Khmer or Pali script, invoking spirits, protective deities, or specific magical intentions. One charm may draw wealth. Another may shield against traffic accidents. A third may strengthen the wearer's sexual stamina or influence. These aren't metaphysical abstractions—they're working talismans. Worn daily. Trusted deeply.

Some are shaped plainly. Others feature animal heads, sharp teeth, or wild faces—amplifiers of specific energies. The carved phallus may be paired with a tiger for dominance, a naga serpent for hidden power, or a monkey for clever charm. These combinations are chosen with care. When someone buys a *Palad Khik*, they're not picking a souvenir. They're choosing a magical ally.

Up in Bhutan, the walls of homes are painted with large, detailed phalluses. Some laugh. Some snarl. Some spit fire. They mark the influence of Lama Drukpa Kunley, who used the phallus as a spiritual weapon. He was known to defeat demons with his wooden wand—not through violence, but through shock, irreverence, and divine authority. He broke illusions and unlocked blessings. He didn't tame desire—he redirected it toward wisdom.

His temple still stands. Women make pilgrimage to receive a blessing—lightly tapped on the head with a wooden phallus carved generations ago. They ask for healing, fertility, or spiritual alignment. The rite isn't a joke. It's a focused prayer, built on centuries of trust. The monks maintain the ritual not out of obligation, but because the work still works.

Now to Japan, where the *Kanamara Matsuri* unfolds each spring. In Kawasaki, giant phalluses are wheeled through the streets, surrounded by crowds, laughter, and reverence. The celebration honors the iron phallus once kept in a local shrine—a tool of protection used by sex workers to guard against illness. Over time, the ritual expanded. Today, it includes prayers for fertility, relationship harmony, and business success.

During the festival, people write wishes on paper slips and tie them to shrines. Couples hold hands and offer thanks. Priests in white robes bless offerings. The energy is festive, yes—but make no mistake, it's also spiritual. The phallus is front and center, not as a prop, but as a sacred participant. And in quiet villages far from the festival, smaller shrines still hold phallic stones or trees wrapped in red cloth, prayed to with incense and simple chants.

What all these cultures show us is that the phallus doesn't need reclaiming in the East—it never lost its place. It was never filtered through the lens of shame. It wasn't reduced to a body part or locked inside gender roles. It remained a working symbol of life-force, of will, of sacred momentum.

And in every case—whether a *lingam*, a *Palad Khik*, or a festival sculpture—it's not about control. It's about connection. When something is stuck, when fertility fails, when danger lingers too long, the phallus is invoked to clear the way. To stand at the edge of the home. To direct energy forward. Not for domination—but for movement. For blessing. For life to begin again.

These symbols are not dead. They still breathe through hands that carve, pray, anoint, and offer. And they remind us that power doesn't always shout. Sometimes it stands. Tall, grounded, and fully awake.

Shiva Lingam stones. Previous page.

Lingam with face of Shiva (Ekamukhalinga), ca. 7th century, Ancient Kingdom of Kashmir, India; Metropolitan Museum of Art, New York City, NY, USA.

Shiva Ekamukhalinga, early 5th century, Mathura, India; Victoria and Albert Museum, London, UK.

FEMALE-CENTERED PHALLIC WORSHIP

To talk about female-centered phallic worship is to enter a conversation that is both sacred and misunderstood. It is a topic that invites us to look deeper—beyond the candle, beyond the shape, and into the living legacy of women's power as sexual, spiritual, and magical beings. Just as there are candles designed in the shape of the vulva to honor feminine desire and manifestation, so too have women used phallic-shaped candles to call down the lightning bolt of divine masculine energy—not as something to tame or possess, but as something to direct.

Let's be honest. While the world has long overemphasized the phallus as a symbol of dominance, control, and ego-driven conquest, female-centered magical traditions have used it differently. Women throughout history have used phallic imagery and objects not for submission, but for activation—of pleasure, of fertility, of creative power. The penis-shaped candle in a woman's hands becomes a wand of invocation. It is not about him. It's about what she is calling into her life, what she chooses to awaken, and what she demands to arrive at her feet, already throbbing with purpose.

In these rituals, the candle becomes a kind of stand-in—not for a specific man, necessarily, but for masculine energy as a whole. In some cases, the candle may be carved with the name of a desired partner. In other cases, it represents the concept of desire itself. The practitioner may dress the candle with oils like "Come to Me," "Follow Me Boy," or "Fire of Love," depending on the purpose of the spell. It might be used to draw forth a lover, ignite a sleeping partnership, or fuel the passion in one's own body after a season of neglect or heartbreak.

Sexual magic, when wielded by women, is often about reclamation. Phallic candles, when used with intention and direction, can become tools of reclamation and manifestation—just as potent as any wand in the hands of a ceremonial magician. A woman may use a red penis candle to stimulate her own libido or to call forth a lover who is both sexually compatible and emotionally connected. She may choose to anoint it with oils made from cinnamon, patchouli, or damiana—herbs associated with arousal, heat, and grounding. These choices aren't arbitrary; they're alchemical. They create a bridge between body and spirit, desire and discipline.

Some may choose to go further and involve their own bodily fluids in the working, applying menstrual blood or vaginal secretions to the candle to charge it with personal power. Others may masturbate with the candle—not for amusement or indulgence, but as a focused magical act of raising energy. The climax becomes the moment of release and intent, sending the spell into the spiritual realm like a flaming arrow shot from the bow of the goddess herself. In those moments, the line between the sacred and the erotic disappears. The body becomes the altar, the candle the offering.

It is worth noting that not all phallic candle use is about desire. Some female practitioners use these candles in reversal spells—to block, banish, or bind a toxic lover, to symbolically sever energetic cords, or to return harmful sexual energy back to its sender. The same tool that invites love can also defend against harm. That's the dual nature of the phallus in spellwork. It can heal or harm, summon or silence. The difference lies in the hands that hold it and the heart that directs its flame.

We must also acknowledge the broader cultural and spiritual traditions that honored phallic power in service of the feminine. In ancient fertility rites, both the lingam and the yoni were worshipped in union. When a woman lights a penis-shaped candle with intention, she's tapping into this lineage, whether she realizes it or not. She is saying, "I will not wait for you to choose me. I will summon you. I will shape you. I will decide what is worthy of entering my sacred space."

This kind of magic requires clarity. It asks the practitioner to be honest about what she wants—not just in bed, but in life. Is she calling in a one-night stand? A soulmate? An apology? Is she seeking justice, passion, or peace? These are not superficial questions. They are the foundation of ethical and effective spellwork.

And while the world may scoff or laugh, the serious practitioner does not. She understands that the shape of a candle is not a joke, but a symbol. Symbols matter. They are the language of the subconscious, the alphabet of the unseen. When she lights that candle, she is not playing. She is conjuring. She is remembering. She is reclaiming.

In the end, female-centered phallic worship is not about the object itself—it's about what that object awakens. It is about calling power back into the body and into the ritual. It's about honoring the sacred marriage of action and receptivity. And it is about knowing, without apology, that the feminine is not passive. She creates, destroys, calls forth, and sends away. And sometimes, she does it with a candle in the shape of a penis, held steady in her hand, lit by her will, and fed by the fire of her own desire.

MEDIEVAL PERCEPTION OF THE PHALLUS

When we think of medieval Europe, we tend to envision gray stone walls, black-robed priests, and endless sermons about sin. This was the era where anything bodily—especially sexual—was immediately suspect, labeled carnal, shameful, or devil-born. And yet, despite all the religious repression, medieval people still carved phalluses into their churches. They etched them into the corners of manuscripts, tucked them into marginalia with a wink, and carried amulets of erect genitals beneath their tunics. If the phallus was the great taboo, it was also a quietly enduring symbol of power, protection, and fertility—right there in the open for anyone with eyes to see.

This contradiction wasn't accidental. It reflected the real spiritual tension of the time. The Christian Church spent much of the medieval era trying to divorce spirit from flesh, heaven from earth, and the sacred from the sexual. But folk belief never quite went along with that plan. The common people— farmers, tradesmen, midwives—knew what the clergy tried to suppress: sex creates life, and life is divine. The phallus, then, wasn't just a body part; it was a magical tool, a force of generative energy, capable of bestowing luck, healing infertility, and warding off evil. It walked that razor-thin line between vulgar and holy.

One of the most curious medieval traditions involved "sheela-na-gigs" and their lesser-discussed male counterparts. While sheela-na-gigs were stone carvings of women displaying exaggerated vulvas, some churches and sacred spaces also included carvings of men holding or pointing to prominent genitalia. These images were sometimes placed over doorways or on the sides of buildings, especially near thresholds, where people crossed from one space into another. That's no coincidence. The doorway is a liminal space, a place of in-between. And what better symbol for protection and vitality than the erect phallus, an image of crossing, of transition, of life breaking through?

We also see this symbolism in the use of fascinum—tiny phallic charms worn to ward off the evil eye. While their origin is Roman, these amulets continued to appear throughout the medieval period, often in Italy and southern France. Some were shaped like simple rods; others had wings, legs, or bells attached. The purpose was the same: to deflect harmful energy, protect against jealousy, and affirm life. People wore them, carried them, and hung them in homes and stables. It wasn't uncommon to see a charm like this dangling from a child's crib or woven into a horse's tack. While the Church may have turned a blind eye to such things in public, these amulets persisted in private, held close to the body like a secret talisman against spiritual attack.

In manuscripts of the era, you'll sometimes find what scholars politely call "grotesques"—little illustrations tucked into the margins of religious texts. These weren't just idle doodles. Some of them were sexually explicit, including drawings of men with enormous erections or comically exaggerated genitalia. Why would a monk, copying sacred scripture, feel the need to draw such things? Maybe it was subversive humor. Maybe it was a spell in disguise. Or maybe, it was an unconscious way to honor the very life force that the text was trying so hard to suppress. In any case, it's clear that the phallus refused to be exiled completely. Even in the cloister, it found a way in.

The medieval obsession with sin often centered around the flesh—particularly male arousal and female temptation. But what gets less attention is how some early medical and religious writings treated the phallus not as shameful, but as a natural barometer of a man's spiritual and physical health. In some texts, impotence was seen as a sign of divine punishment. In others, it was a sign of magical interference—often blamed on women, of course, who were believed to use charms or potions to "bind" a man's virility. This led to the rise of "unbinding" rituals—magical or religious cures designed to restore potency and remove hexes. A candle shaped like a phallus might be lit for this purpose, dressed with specific oils and prayers to restore a man's "uprightness," both physically and morally.

There's also a peculiar overlap between medieval medicine and folk magic, particularly around what was called "sympathetic magic." According to this theory, you could influence a person by manipulating something that resembled the part of the body you wanted to affect. This is where we see the use of carved phallic wood or other long objects. A woman who wanted her husband to remain sexually loyal might bury such an item under the threshold of their home. A midwife trying to ensure fertility might wear a charm shaped like a penis or create a potion containing herbs associated with male potency. These were not crude jokes—they were acts of spiritual intention, rooted in ancient understandings of how the physical and metaphysical worlds mirror each other.

Despite the Church's efforts to shame and sanitize, folk culture held fast to the understanding that sexuality, fertility, and sacred power were all threads of the same tapestry. The phallus, far from being a simple obscenity, was a loaded symbol of life, power, vulnerability, and spiritual potency. And even in the darkest corners of repression, it continued to show up—in carvings, in amulets, in whispered spells—asserting its place in the sacred and profane alike.

So when we talk about magical objects or symbols from the medieval world, let's not overlook the power that was placed on the body itself. The phallus was a signpost, a sigil, a talisman—sometimes feared, sometimes mocked, often hidden—but never fully erased. It carried more than just crude meaning. It was a stand-in for life force, a defiance against spiritual sterilization, and a reminder that even in the most pious of times, magic still clung to the flesh.

RENAISSANCE AND RENEWED INTEREST

By the time the Renaissance bloomed across Europe, the world had changed dramatically. We had gone from tribal fires and pagan festivals to city squares, universities, and cathedrals that loomed like mountains over the people. But with all its advancements in art, science, and literature, the Renaissance didn't shake its fascination with love magic. If anything, it elevated it. This was a time when love spells moved from the hands of the common folk into the grip of the upper class—wealthy merchants, landowners, and even clergy were known to dabble discreetly. While love magic had always existed, it took on a new form during this period: calculated, cunning, and cloaked in the veil of religious respectability.

What makes this era so compelling is the sheer duality of it. On one hand, the Church wielded more power than ever, condemning sorcery as heresy. On the other, people were quietly slipping spells into altar crevices, lighting sacred candles with ulterior motives, and even stealing the consecrated Host to include in their magical workings. It was spiritual espionage at its finest. Pagan magic didn't disappear—it learned to wear Christian robes.

During this time, love spells were not frivolous pursuits. They were strategic. These rituals were often aimed at securing marriage, not mere flirtation. This was a period when marriage meant elevation—access to land, status, and power. In a society built on inheritance and alliances, love magic was used to override the constraints of birth and class. You weren't just trying to get someone to notice you; you were trying to rewrite your future.

One example comes from the poetic works of William Langland, who wrote about a woman so determined to be with her true love that she arranged the death of her wealthy husband. Another of his poems describes a jilted lover crying out, "Your laughter will return to me." Whether literal or symbolic, these words read like the echo of a spell, spoken with the desperate certainty of someone who refused to let go.

This period also gave rise to an unfortunate belief—that women were the main culprits behind magic. The infamous *Malleus Maleficarum*, published in 1487, claimed that "all witchcraft comes from carnal lust, which in women is insatiable." It tied women's sexuality directly to sorcery, branding them as natural-born temptresses whose very bodies were doorways to the devil. The book painted menstruation, childbirth, and even romantic longing as dangerous forces. And so, women who dared to practice magic—especially love magic—risked being cast as witches simply for wanting affection or agency.

But that didn't stop them.

The Renaissance woman who cast a love spell was not a fool. She understood the risk. She lit her candles in secret, buried her charm bags beneath floorboards, and whispered incantations in silence. She knew what was at stake. If her magic worked, she secured a future she might otherwise have been denied. If it failed, she risked scorn—or worse. But the potential reward outweighed the risk.

Christian symbolism also became entangled with spellwork during this era. Candles from the church altar were repurposed for love rituals. Spell scrolls were tucked into the crevices of sacred statues. Some even pilfered relics or scraps from communion tables, believing the spiritual energy imbued in them could intensify their spells. There's a kind of poetic rebellion in that—a merging of sacred and profane, of divine love and earthly desire.

What this era teaches us is simple: love magic never really died. It just adapted. It found new ways to breathe, even under scrutiny. In the glow of a cathedral candle or the margins of a handwritten psalm, love spells lived on. And the people casting them weren't only chasing romance—they were chasing control, connection, and sometimes, survival.

The Renaissance did not mark the return of love magic—it revealed that it had never gone away. It had simply learned to hide better. Beneath the surface of every sermon and psalm was someone, somewhere, asking for love to come, stay, or return. And they weren't just praying. They were doing the work.

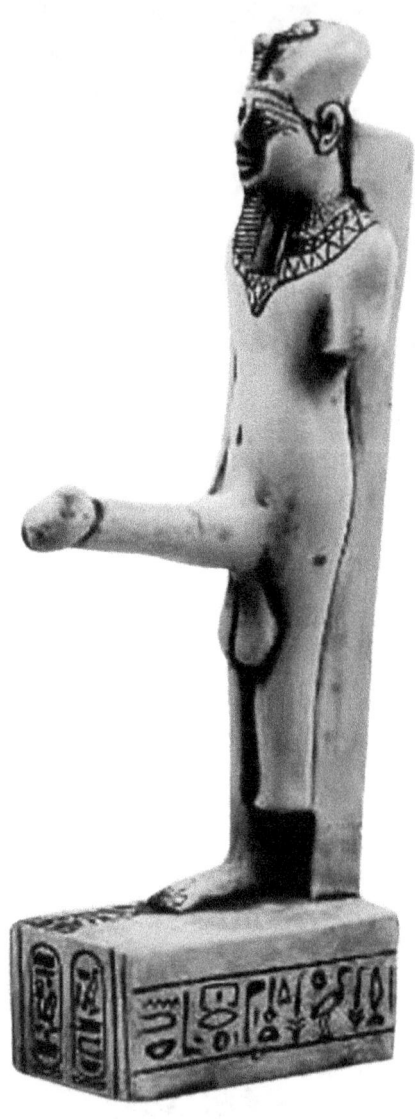

An Egyptian fertility god

THE PHALLUS IN FOLKLORE AND MYTHS

No matter the century, no matter the continent, people have always had something to say about the penis. Whether honored as a sacred emblem of life force or treated as a taboo joke whispered behind fans and veils, it's clear that this one body part carries more symbolic weight than perhaps any other. Entire mythologies have been built around it, entire curses and blessings bestowed through it, and, in some cultures, entire deities were reduced to—or elevated as—nothing more than a divine phallus.

Let's start with the gods. In ancient Egypt, the story of Osiris tells of his murder and dismemberment by his jealous brother Set. Isis, his wife, reassembled his body, but the one piece she could not find was his penis. So, she fashioned one from gold and resurrected him long enough to conceive Horus. Think about that: the myth hinges on the magical, divine importance of the phallus—not just as a physical part of the body but as a spiritual tool of continuation and resurrection. Gold, of course, represents perfection, incorruptibility, and eternal power. So even in its symbolic replacement, the phallus became the centerpiece of creation. It wasn't just about sex. It was about lineage, legacy, and sacred power.

Over in Greece, Dionysus—the god of wine, ecstasy, and chaos—was paraded in processions where large phalluses were carried through the streets, celebrated and venerated. This wasn't crude. It was religious.

The phallus was seen as a force of fertility and wild, raw life. And in Rome, the fascinum—a carved or cast image of an erect penis—was worn or displayed to ward off the evil eye. These weren't tucked away in drawers. They hung openly around children's necks and were placed on household altars. In fact, the phallic amulet was considered one of the most potent forms of protection in the Roman world.

These were cultures that understood something many modern minds forget: that symbolism and reverence can be held in the same hand. The penis wasn't merely an instrument of lust or a source of shame. It was a talisman, a protector, a symbol of masculine divine energy. That idea held strong across Europe, where even the Celts carved phallic symbols into standing stones, believing them to be blessings of the land itself.

But the phallus didn't just appear in sacred sculpture. It made its way into folk tales, cautionary stories, and even children's rhymes—though often buried in metaphor. Consider the tale of the "green man," a symbol of virility and seasonal rebirth, whose foliage-covered form graces cathedrals across Britain and Europe. While some see only leaves and vines, others recognize the not-so-subtle nod to the hidden male anatomy, bursting forth in spring, seeding the land, then dying back come winter. The natural cycle was never seen as gender-neutral—it was intentionally masculine and feminine, working in tandem. The phallus was the spark, the fire, the sacred ignition of the wheel of life.

In hoodoo, the phallus shows up less as myth and more as material. The raccoon penis bone, or "coon dong," is a classic Southern curiosity, worn as a charm to attract lovers, ensure male virility, or bring dominance in the bedroom. This wasn't just folk superstition—it was often seen as practical magic. Men carried them in mojo bags for luck with women, while women used them in spells to make their man stay home, stay hard, and stay faithful. Once again, the phallus wasn't just about sex; it was about control, power, and security—whether spiritual or physical.

Across African diasporic traditions, phallic symbols are still used to represent male deities of force and potency. In Haitian Vodou, for instance, Papa Legba is often associated with the crossroads and is sometimes symbolized with a phallic staff—though interpretations vary widely across houses and lineages. In Congo-derived traditions, nkisi figures often carry a prominent phallus as a sign of forceful magic and dynamic action. These images weren't ornamental. They were functional. The carved wood, the iron spikes, the protruding organ—they were part of an entire system of sympathetic magic. What you carve into form, you give life to in spirit.

Of course, it wasn't always celebratory. Many cautionary tales involved men who misused their power and paid for it dearly. In various folk stories, the punishment for philandering, assault, or betrayal was often symbolically tied to the phallus. From stories of impotence to tales of severed anatomy, folklore made it clear: the phallus may be a gift, but it comes with responsibility. Abuse it, and it will betray you.

This duality shows up even in more modern cultural superstitions. The fear of "losing one's manhood" or being rendered impotent by a curse still runs deep in some communities. Hexes aimed at sexual dysfunction are some of the oldest and most persistent in folk magic. The reason? Because people understood, whether consciously or not, that sexuality and vitality were deeply connected. If you could control a man's sex life, you could control much more than that—you could control his sense of self, his confidence, his power in the world.

So when we look at the phallus in myth and folklore, we're not just seeing a body part. We're seeing a symbol that has been loaded with centuries of reverence, fear, control, celebration, shame, and sacredness. From ancient temples to hoodoo mojo bags, it has played the role of god, monster, protector, and destroyer. And like all things in magic, its meaning shifts with context, culture, and intention.

Whether carved in stone or lit in wax, the phallus continues to occupy a central role in magical thought—not because it is lewd or obscene, but because it is powerful. Folklore teaches us again and again that power—any power—must be wielded with wisdom. And so, the stories continue. The myths expand. And the magic, like the symbol itself, rises and endures.

MODERN INTERPRETATIONS OF PHALLIC SYMBOLS

As society has progressed through waves of liberation and suppression, the way we view the phallus has changed significantly. Once carved into sacred stones or worn on leather cords as protective amulets, it now shows up on novelty items, graffiti walls, and even high-end fashion runways. But the spiritual and symbolic power of the phallus hasn't disappeared—it's simply been translated, repackaged, and sometimes distorted to fit modern narratives. What was once revered as a sacred shape with deep magical and generative power has, in many ways, become something humorous, taboo, or aggressively sexualized. So let's dig into the many ways this ancient form still influences us—whether we recognize it or not.

In contemporary spiritual practices, particularly those influenced by Paganism, Wicca, and modern witchcraft, the phallus is still used to represent the divine masculine—the counterpart to the womb or chalice, which represents the divine feminine. Together, they are understood as symbols of balance, not opposition. The masculine brings force, direction, protection, and generative energy. The feminine brings receptivity, creation, intuition, and nurturance. You'll often find these two energies mirrored in ritual tools: the athame (a ritual blade) for masculine energy, and the cauldron or chalice for feminine. When used together in ceremony, they reenact the ancient drama of sacred union. This isn't about gender. It's about archetypal energy. And understanding how these symbols play together is the key to unlocking both spiritual balance and personal empowerment.

Phallic imagery also shows up in some surprising places. Think about skyscrapers that reach into the heavens—monuments of power and ambition, designed to dominate the skyline and show off human achievement. Is that not a modern obelisk? Architects may not call it sacred, but the intention behind these structures—asserting presence, dominance, and vision—still echoes ancient impulses. The difference is we no longer bow to the building and ask for rain. In pop culture, phallic symbols are often used for shock value or humor, but even in those moments, they are subconsciously tapping into old archetypes. We laugh, we blush, we look away—but somewhere deep in the psyche, the message gets received. Symbols work that way. They don't need our permission to function.

Modern artists, especially those interested in exploring identity, power, or sexuality, continue to use the phallus in their work. It can be a statement of pride, a rebellion against shame, or a commentary on toxic masculinity. And while not all of it is sacred, much of it is purposeful. Context is everything. Whether something is magical, vulgar, or empowering often depends on the eye of the beholder—and the intent of the maker.

Within modern magical practices, penis candles and related imagery are still widely used—not just for love and lust, but also for power, domination, and spiritual justice. As discussed earlier, these forms can be dressed, carved, and consecrated for a variety of workings. But the shape remains relevant because the energetic principle it represents hasn't changed. It's still the seed. The spark. The force that presses forward, creates change, and makes things happen. You don't need to return to the temple of Priapus to understand that.

The presence of phallic shapes in modern branding and design should not be overlooked, either. From product packaging to logos, sharp upward forms are often used to convey strength, virility, and ambition. Think about the way some car brands design their grilles and hoods to look fast, sleek, and strong. There's a reason power tools, weapons, and even sports drinks are marketed with these shapes and symbols. The language of the phallus is still being spoken—it's just being used in marketing departments and advertising boards instead of sacred groves and altars.

And while some people may roll their eyes at phallic motifs or dismiss them as relics of an outdated worldview, others are beginning to reclaim them with new intention. Some feminist and queer artists are exploring phallic symbols in ways that challenge old hierarchies and reclaim agency. In these hands, the phallus becomes less about dominance and more about creativity, confidence, and sovereignty. That, too, is sacred.

We also see a resurgence in spiritual movements that intentionally revisit ancient symbolism to bring balance back into modern life. Whether through rituals that honor the divine masculine or through guided visualizations that involve awakening sexual energy, the shape and spirit of the phallus remains a powerful trigger for transformation. Tantric and kundalini traditions in particular emphasize the union of masculine and feminine energies in the body, using breath, movement, and meditation to awaken the inner fire. This isn't new. It's just been repackaged.

Phallic symbols, both literal and abstract, are still very much with us. They shape the world we live in, from the art we consume to the architecture that surrounds us. But they also continue to live in our dreams, our rituals, and our creative impulses. And whether we're lighting a candle in the shape of a penis, gazing at a towering monument, or carving a symbol into a spell petition, we're participating in an unbroken thread of human expression that stretches back thousands of years.

So, before you dismiss the symbol as silly or outdated, consider this: something doesn't stay with us this long unless it still has power. And maybe—just maybe—it's not the symbol that needs to change. Maybe it's the way we've been taught to see it.

THE PHALLUS IN PSYCHOANALYSIS

When modern psychology stepped out from behind the pulpit and tried to explain the soul with science, it didn't take long before it circled right back to one of the oldest magical symbols of them all: the phallus. But unlike ancient priests who carved it into sacred stone or witches who lit candles in its shape, psychoanalysts looked inward. They stripped the symbol of incense and altar and laid it bare across dreams, neuroses, and childhood wounds. And what they found, intentionally or not, was what magical practitioners already knew—that the phallus is never just about flesh. It's a living glyph of will, power, fear, longing, and identity. And in the psyche, it holds even more sway than it does in the body.

Freud was the first to say it aloud—though he spoke with the clinical chill of a surgeon, not the reverent tone of a conjure doctor. To him, the phallus was central to how identity formed. Boys feared losing it; girls supposedly envied it. The "Oedipus complex" he introduced wasn't just about parental dynamics—it was a symbolic ritual of initiation, where the child comes to understand limits, punishment, and desire through the lens of the phallus. According to Freud, you either identified with it, or you spent your life trying to reclaim what you thought you lacked.

Now, we can argue—and many have—about how deeply flawed these theories are, especially in their view of gender and desire. But what can't be denied is this: the phallus, in Freud's model, was never just anatomy. It was status. Symbol. Signifier. A holy object of psychic weight that dictated how people saw themselves in the world, and how they moved through it.

Jung took this even deeper. He saw the phallus not as an individual obsession, but as an archetype—a shared symbol living in the collective unconscious. In his vision, the phallus was an expression of the animus, the inner masculine energy present in all people regardless of gender. The animus speaks to direction, will, logic, movement, assertion. And in dreams, that energy often appears as a sword, a wand, a tower, or yes—a penis. These aren't random. They're encoded messages from the soul. The phallus, in this context, points not to sexuality but to action. Integration. Awakening.

If you've ever had a dream where a rod broke, or a tower fell, or a weapon failed to work, you've felt this energy. The broken phallus in dreamwork often signals a fear of impotence—not sexually, but spiritually. A loss of direction. A struggle with power. The rod doesn't rise, and so nothing moves forward. These aren't just symbols. They're symptoms. And the magician—like the analyst—must learn to read them with care.

Jacques Lacan, later in the psychoanalytic lineage, took a more abstract route. He claimed "the phallus is a signifier of desire"—not a thing, but the thing that stands in for everything else. To Lacan, the phallus was the placeholder for what we long for, what we chase, what we perform. It had less to do with organs and more to do with language, absence, and recognition. Again, the language may be academic, but the concept? It's spiritual. It's magical. The phallus as a cipher for will—seen, unseen, and misunderstood.

Now here's where it gets interesting for magical workers. Psychoanalysis, in trying to explain human behavior, accidentally affirmed the very principles folk magicians already understood. The phallus isn't powerful because of what it is—it's powerful because of what we believe it does. That belief, whether conscious or not, creates results. Which is exactly how magic works.

When you light a red penis candle to draw a lover, you're not casting a spell on a body part. You're calling on the psychic charge that part of the body carries. You're invoking centuries of longing, desire, fertility, shame, control, confidence, vulnerability— all wrapped into one charged, symbolic form. The candle becomes a mirror of the unconscious. And the work you do with it ripples far beyond the wax.

This is why phallic symbols in magic aren't bound by gender. In both psychological and magical terms, the phallus belongs to the person wielding it. You don't have to be male to possess phallic energy. You need focus. You need clarity. You need intent. Whether you carry a physical phallus, visualize it in ritual, or wield it through a tool like a wand or blade, what matters is not the flesh—but the force behind it.

Even trauma has a say here. For many, the phallus isn't neutral—it's a wound, a weapon, a symbol of something taken or feared. In therapy, this gets untangled through talk, dreams, shadow work. In magic, we might use cleansing rites, cut-and-clear spells, or reclaiming rituals to remove the stain of what was misused. Because just like in the psyche, in spiritual work the phallus must be understood before it can be safely wielded.

That's the lesson psychoanalysis helps reinforce: the phallus, like any symbol of power, demands interpretation. It's not static. It's not simple. It's a living form that adapts, mutates, and speaks in the language of whoever's holding it. It can be sacred, destructive, redemptive, or repressed. It can speak to confidence—or signal its collapse. But it is never meaningless.

So whether you encounter it in a dream, in a ritual, or in your healing work, don't flinch. Ask what it's trying to show you. Ask what it wants you to reclaim. Because if you meet the phallus in the mind with the same reverence you give it in magic, you'll find it's not just a symbol of sex or strength. It's a symbol of movement. Of knowing. Of choosing. And if you're willing to do the work—to engage the symbol consciously and ethically—then the wand still works. It always did.

PHALLIC TOOLS IN MAGIC AND RITUAL

In folk magic, tools are never just props. They're extensions of will, intention, and energy. Every curve, corner, and crafted detail tells a story, holds a charge, or shapes a specific kind of power. Phallic tools—those shaped like the penis—have been used across cultures and magical systems for centuries. Not because of shock value, but because the phallus has always symbolized the raw, generative force of life.

The penis candle isn't just about sex. It's about power. Not control-over-you kind of power, but primal life-force power—the kind that commands, attracts, penetrates, and ignites. These candles are frequently used in spells of lust, domination, attraction, and sometimes even destruction, depending on how they're handled. Like any magical tool, it's about intention. Stroke it with tenderness, and you're calling in desire. Dress it in oils like Commanding or Domination, and you've just shifted into a higher gear.

Some practitioners shy away from phallic imagery because it feels too explicit or provocative. But in ritual, symbolism is the language we speak. A sword can cut, but it can also defend. A key can open, but it can just as easily lock. The same is true for the phallic candle. It can create or destroy, attract or repel, depending on the hands doing the working.

You'll most often find penis candles molded in red, black, or white. Red is for lust, pure and simple. It stirs up the blood and gets the heart (and other organs) pumping. Black, when used in baneful work, can be used to stop someone's sexual appetite altogether—maybe because they're cheating, maybe because they're bothering you. White is more subtle, often used for healing sexual wounds or softening emotional intimacy that's tied to physical expression.

Engraving the name of your target along the shaft is standard. Some will carve symbols or phrases into it, whispering their intentions into the wax. Others go a step further, adding bodily fluids, hair, or items tied to the person they want to influence. The key here is that you're not just using a candle—you're animating it. You're giving it life, purpose, direction.

For spellwork rooted in attraction or seduction, I often recommend warming the candle between your palms before anointing it. The heat from your hands begins a physical bond. Then, choose your oil with care. Passion Oil, Lust, Follow Me Boy—each oil brings its own flavor to the spell. Begin at the base and stroke upward if you want to bring someone to you. If you're trying to push someone away, stroke downward from the tip toward the base. This reversal of flow is symbolic of repelling, detaching, or shutting down desire.

Another technique is to tie a thread or piece of red yarn around the base and slowly wind it upward with each whispered command. Each wrap can hold a word, a desire, or an image. This turns the candle into a kind of spell-bound effigy. You can even combine it with a petition paper placed underneath, or fold a photo of your target and rest the candle directly on top of it—especially powerful when done over several nights.

Phallic tools don't always need to be candles. Statues, carved wooden phalluses, even crystal ones, are often kept on altars as a symbol of masculine energy. In ancient Roman homes, the fascinum—a winged phallus—was hung by doorways to ward off evil and jealousy. The same charm is still sold today in shops across Italy and carried as a protective amulet. In that context, the phallus is apotropaic. Not erotic. It deflects the evil eye and safeguards the household.

In tantric and Eastern traditions, the phallus—known as the lingam—is honored as sacred. It represents Shiva, the masculine principle, and is balanced by the yoni, the divine feminine. This isn't just symbolism—it's a cosmic principle: creation and destruction, active and receptive, divine and manifest.

When we use phallic tools in our rituals, we're tapping into that deep, ancient current. We're reaching back through time to when magic wasn't separated from the body, when the sacred and the sensual were one and the same. That doesn't mean we have to be explicit for the sake of being edgy. It means we respect the power of form and function. If you blush while dressing a penis candle but still light it anyway, you're doing it right. It means you recognize the seriousness of what you're invoking. Humor may be part of it—but the work is still the work.

Just remember: the candle burns whether you're laughing or crying. And the spell will still work. It's not about whether the shape makes you uncomfortable. It's about whether you understand the tool, what it represents, and how you're choosing to wield it.

So whether you're using a phallic candle to light the fires of lust, push away an unwanted lover, or channel commanding energy into your target, do it with focus and respect. Because in the world of folk magic, symbols are never just objects. They're contracts. They're keys. And sometimes, they're shaped like a cock because that's the language our ancestors spoke to get the job done.

Let your tools be deliberate, your hands steady, and your intention clear. Power, after all, is best handled by those who understand what it is they're holding.

PHALLIC SYMBOLISM IN ABRAHAMIC RELIGIONS

When we turn our attention to Abrahamic religions—Judaism, Christianity, and Islam—we're met with a paradox. On one hand, these faiths shaped entire civilizations and remain central to the spiritual lives of billions. On the other, they also bear the weight of complex cultural taboos around sex, gender, and bodily autonomy. It is within this paradox that we must examine the role and representation of the phallus—not just as an anatomical feature but as a deep symbol of covenant, power, purity, and even divine promise.

Let's begin with Judaism, where one of the most unmistakable phallic rites is found in the act of circumcision. In Genesis 17, God commands Abraham to circumcise himself, his son Ishmael, and every male in his household. This act, known as *brit milah*, is more than a health practice or rite of passage—it is a visible and permanent mark of the covenant between the Hebrew people and their God. It transforms the phallus into a literal signature of divine agreement. The idea that a sacred promise can be etched into the flesh speaks volumes about how powerfully the phallic symbol operates within this religious framework. It isn't about shame—it's about identity, belonging, and commitment. And it's blood-bound.

In Christianity, things get more complicated. The early church, influenced heavily by Greco-Roman culture and ascetic ideals, quickly distanced itself from overt expressions of sexuality. As the theology developed, the body—and especially the male member—became more associated with temptation and sin rather than sacredness. Yet, the very idea of the Word made flesh—Jesus Christ incarnate—is a deeply embodied, physical manifestation of divine essence. While we don't find direct phallic rites like in Judaism, the undercurrent of divine masculinity, lineage, and generational continuity runs deep.

Consider the emphasis on Christ's genealogy in the Gospels. The "begats" listed in Matthew are not there for light reading; they are a meticulous tracing of male lineage, signifying divine legitimacy. The unspoken implication is the potency of the male line—not just in terms of inheritance, but in spiritual authority. Though veiled, it is still a form of symbolic phallic continuity, masked by the language of ancestry and spiritual succession.

And then there's the cross. While it is not a phallic symbol in the traditional sense, its vertical orientation and its association with sacrifice, suffering, and redemption give it a masculine charge that should not be overlooked. The cross is wood, erect, and planted into the earth—a structure that connects heaven and earth, spirit and flesh, death and resurrection. It is a bridge between worlds, much like the phallus has been seen in earlier fertility cults and mystery religions. Symbolism doesn't always arrive in neon signs. Sometimes it comes cloaked in metaphor, in ritual, or in silence.

In Islam, circumcision also plays a central role. Though not directly mentioned in the Qur'an, the practice is widely observed among Muslims as a prophetic tradition (*sunnah*), said to have been passed down from the Prophet Ibrahim—Abraham, once again. This is important because it mirrors the Judaic covenant, reinforcing the idea that physical alteration of the male organ serves a divine purpose. Islam's regard for bodily cleanliness and purity only strengthens this association. The male organ isn't a source of shame, but it is something to be regulated, marked, and purified.

Yet Islam, much like Christianity, shrouds sexual imagery beneath layers of modesty, discipline, and prescribed roles. That said, within Sufi poetry and mysticism, we find a much more open celebration of union, longing, and even erotic metaphor as a pathway to divine connection. In those texts, union with the divine is often described in language that can easily be interpreted through a symbolic sexual lens. The beloved becomes the object of desire, the seeker the passionate lover. The boundaries between sacred longing and sensual yearning blur—and while the imagery may be subtle, the energy is unmistakable.

It's important to acknowledge that in all three of these religious systems, the male body is simultaneously elevated and constrained. Its generative power is recognized, but also heavily monitored. Its symbolic weight is immense, but its physical expression is often pushed into the shadows of taboo. Even where the phallus is sanctified—as in the covenant of circumcision—it is done through the act of wounding, cutting, and consecrating. This reveals something deeper about Abrahamic thought: the sacred is rarely unmarked. It often comes through blood, suffering, or sacrifice.

So, what does this tell us as magical practitioners or spiritual thinkers? First, that symbolism doesn't vanish just because a culture says it shouldn't be spoken of. The phallus never disappeared from these religions—it just changed its shape, its language, and its mode of expression. It became the rod of Moses that parted the sea. It became the tower in a dream. It became the tree rooted in holy ground. The energy remains—it simply migrated into new forms.

Second, this reinforces the truth that magical symbols are not exclusive to one tradition or time period. The phallus, in all its forms, lives at the crossroads of power, spirit, creation, and identity. Whether it's carved into ancient fertility idols or hidden in the structure of patriarchal theology, it continues to speak. But only to those with ears to hear.

And finally, we're reminded that the deeper we explore the spiritual frameworks of our ancestors— across culture and faith—the more we begin to see that even in the most conservative traditions, the body remains a vessel of sacred meaning. Not in spite of its physicality, but because of it. The divine has always found ways to leave its mark. Sometimes it's in the sky, sometimes in the heart—but often, it's right there in the body, carved in flesh, passed through blood, and buried in symbol.

PHALLIC TREE WORSHIP AND NATURAL SYMBOLISM

All over the world, people have honored the connection between the divine and the natural world through trees. And not just any tree—those with a certain upright, reaching posture were often seen as more than wood and leaves. They were considered embodiments of fertility, life, and cosmic connection. In cultures both ancient and indigenous, the tree stood as a living symbol of the phallus—not for laughs or shock, but as a sacred image of the power to create.

This symbolic connection didn't appear by accident. A tree grows straight up from the earth and reaches toward the heavens. It is rooted in soil but rises skyward, which mirrors the human body and spirit— the grounded self and the spiritual self striving for connection. It is both masculine in its upright thrust and feminine in its capacity to bear fruit. The phallic tree is not only a masculine symbol; it is a unifier of opposites, a full expression of the generative principle in nature.

In Greek mythology, the pine tree was sacred to Attis, a god associated with fertility and vegetation. Roman rituals to Cybele, the mother of the Gods, involved parading a pine tree as a phallic stand-in for the god's lost genitals—yes, they went there. But it wasn't scandalous. It was mournful and reverent. That tree represented the masculine force of life itself, cut down and reborn, again and again, with the seasons.

In India, the lingam is a familiar stone symbol representing Shiva, the god of destruction and rebirth. While often misunderstood in the West, the lingam is not crude or vulgar. It is an abstract form that speaks to the power of masculine energy as a life-giver, and it is frequently installed in temples under or near sacred trees. Together, the tree and the stone become a ritual landscape of fertility and transcendence.

The Norse Yggdrasil, the World Tree, was imagined as a cosmic pillar connecting the heavens, the earthly plane, and the underworld. It was no accident that this "axis mundi" had a shape that echoed the human spine and a towering, upright form. From this tree, Odin was said to have hung himself, sacrificing himself to himself to gain wisdom. Yggdrasil was both the container of life and a channel of sacrifice—life, death, and rebirth, all in one symbol.

Even in Christian tradition, the Tree of Life and the Tree of Knowledge of Good and Evil in the Garden of Eden are archetypal symbols that echo ancient tree worship. The biblical stories often replaced earlier fertility myths but kept their structure. The tree in Eden became a place of awakening and change. And like many myths before it, it stood at the center of human experience—the place where innocence ends and awareness begins.

Throughout the centuries, many folk traditions—especially in rural parts of Europe—have carried on phallic tree rites long after the rise of Christianity. Maypoles, still popular in spring festivals across the continent, are perhaps the most obvious example.

The tall pole is planted in the earth, adorned with flowers and ribbons, and danced around in circles. Fertility is evoked with joy, music, and movement. The Maypole, though sterilized in modern times, was once a clear ritual of earth and body, sex and seed.

Other tree rituals have included planting fruit trees to increase fertility in women, hanging cloth ribbons on sacred branches to send prayers or attract lovers, or even dancing naked under specific trees to call in virility or abundance. There are folk stories where lovers consummate relationships in groves, believing that doing so will make their bond stronger and their union blessed by the spirits of the woods.

Some Hoodoo and conjure traditions carry a deep respect for trees, especially those known to be "spirit trees." In the South, the cedar tree was often seen as protective and male in nature, while the willow carried feminine, emotional energy. But when it came to desire, strength, and conjuring the powers of life and death, practitioners turned to trees like the oak— bold, unshakable, and long-lived. Pieces of bark or root from certain trees were carried as potent charms, especially when gathered in ritual ways or at specific times.

It's important to remember that symbolism is not just about the object—it's about how people relate to it. A tree might be a tree to the modern eye, but to the wise, it is an ancient witness to everything: storms and sunshine, births and burials, unions and betrayals. The tree has seen it all and holds the power of memory within its rings.

In magical practice today, you can still work with trees in deeply symbolic ways. If you're doing love or fertility work, consider performing your ritual at the base of a strong, living tree. Whisper your desires into its trunk. Tie your petition to a branch with thread. Bury an offering at its roots. You are engaging with a living altar that carries the energy of generations.

Ultimately, the phallic tree is not about sex alone—it's about life. It's about the divine spark that reaches upward and the grounded strength that holds firm. It is the body and the spirit, the symbol and the source. To recognize the sacred in the form of a tree is to recognize the sacred in your own form—the potential to grow, reach, endure, and renew.

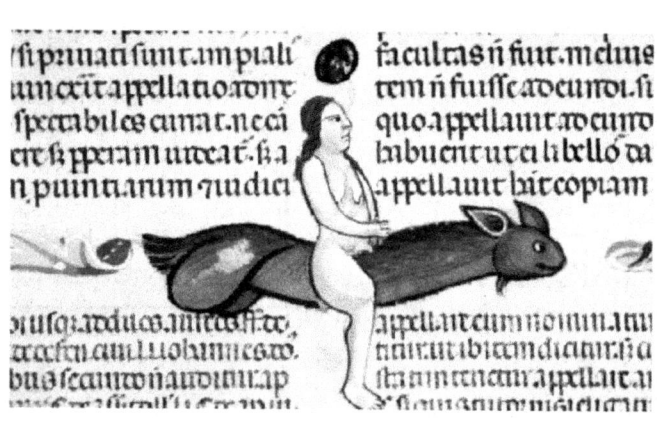

THE EVOLUTION OF PHALLIC WORSHIP IN MODERN ESOTERIC TRADITIONS

The sacred phallus didn't disappear from magical practice—it adapted. What once stood in the open air of temples and public altars has, in modern times, been pushed into the back rooms of metaphysical shops, discreetly sold as candles, oils, or hidden behind clever product names. The symbol still carries spiritual power and significance, but society's discomfort with sexuality, particularly male sexuality, has transformed it into something whispered about rather than revered. In truth, much of the modern magical world is still shaped by a Victorian hangover—obsessed with appearances, constantly sanitizing the raw power of sex into more palatable language.

In contemporary pagan and esoteric circles, the phallus quietly makes its way into ritual through tools, language, and symbolic gesture. The athame, for example, is a phallic instrument—used in many Wiccan rituals to direct energy, represent the masculine principle, and "plunge" into the chalice during the Great Rite, a symbolic sexual union that represents divine balance and creation. But rarely do we talk openly about what's really happening. The Great Rite is a reenactment of sexual union, yes, but it's also a prayer for fertility, vitality, and universal harmony. It's the phallus and womb reunited through ritual—and yet we rarely say so out loud.

The move toward symbolic euphemism isn't limited to tools. In ceremonial magic, especially traditions rooted in the Hermetic Order of the Golden Dawn or Thelema, phallic imagery is often dressed in astrological or alchemical garb. It becomes Mars, sulfur, or fire. We trade in metaphors—sometimes for modesty, sometimes to protect the uninitiated— but the underlying structure remains rooted in the same ancient reverence. Aleister Crowley didn't shy away from sexual symbolism in his work, and many of his rituals leaned heavily on the power of the erect phallus as an engine of magical will. But the average reader of his texts may miss that entirely, distracted by layers of poetic abstraction and coded language.

In modern Tantra, which has been adapted and often misunderstood in the West, the phallus is known as the lingam. Rather than shame or hide it, traditional Tantric practice views the lingam as a divine tool of consciousness and transformation. In sacred union, the lingam and yoni meet not just as flesh but as conduits of cosmic energy. The body becomes temple. Sex becomes ceremony. And through this, the practitioner moves closer to enlightenment. It's a theology of the body that stands in stark contrast to the guilt-based teachings of many Western religions.

Meanwhile, in folk magic and Hoodoo, the influence of the phallus tends to show up in more practical ways. Penis candles, for instance, are used in spells of control, seduction, and energy domination—not always for romantic purposes, but sometimes for business, influence, or even courtroom work. One conjure worker I knew used a black penis candle not for revenge or lust, but to dominate the energy in a legal dispute. She fixed it with Court Case oil, carved the names of the opposing party along the shaft, and burned it over a mixture of slippery elm and licorice root. The symbolism wasn't erotic—it was strategic. She wasn't appealing to sex. She was commanding influence. She wanted her words to carry weight and her opponent's arguments to go limp. And they did.

That's the nature of this kind of work. You take a form charged with meaning, and you re-aim it. The candle becomes a stand-in for power itself. Not about body—but about will. About impact. That's why these tools have lasted: they work when they're used with precision and clarity.

Of course, the spiritual significance of the phallus has also been distorted and misused. Some modern occult groups have veered into toxic masculinity or fetishized dominance under the guise of divine masculinity. This is where discernment is essential. Not everything that calls itself "sacred" is holy. When reverence turns into entitlement or domination becomes abuse, it is no longer magic—it is harm wearing a mask. The sacred masculine is not about power over others, but power in alignment with creation, balance, and respect for all life.

It's also worth noting how the rise of queer magic has reshaped phallic symbolism. In gay male magical circles, for example, there is often a reclamation of the phallus not as a symbol of dominance, but as a source of connection, vulnerability, and mutual pleasure. The phallus becomes a bridge rather than a weapon—still sacred, still powerful, but liberated from the heteronormative lens. In this context, sex magic isn't about conquest. It's about communion. It's about crafting space for desire, authenticity, and the sacred nature of queer bodies.

As modern practitioners, we get to decide how we engage with this symbolism. Do we hide it, dress it up in polite language, or do we speak plainly about its role in our magical systems? When we light a candle shaped like a penis, when we plunge an athame into a chalice, or when we invoke a deity like Pan, Min, or Priapus—we are engaging with an ancient current. The current of life itself. Phallic worship isn't about idolizing the flesh. It's about understanding the energy that flows through it, the stories it carries, and the spiritual legacy it represents.

In the end, the evolution of phallic worship in modern esotericism reflects the evolution of our own thinking. We've moved from open veneration to veiled symbolism, from temples to toolboxes, from shame to sacred reclamation. Whether you work with it as fire, sword, wand, or candle, the message remains: the creative spark is within you, and it waits to be honored. Not with embarrassment or avoidance, but with intention, clarity, and the wisdom to know when to wield it and when to let it rest.

USING THE PHALLUS IN MAGIC SPELLS

The phallus is not just a symbol. It is a tool. A channel. A force. And in the hands of a skilled practitioner, it becomes a living conduit for magical action—whether crafted from candle wax, carved into wood, worn as a charm, or awakened within the body itself. To work phallic magic is to work with raw, directional energy—the will that moves outward, penetrates, commands, and transforms.

Phallic magic can be gentle or aggressive, seductive or protective. It can be used to bring in lovers, inspire courage, bless new ventures, or banish harm. But no matter the goal, the key is intention. The practitioner must charge the phallus—whether physical or symbolic—with focused will. Like all magic, this is not about superstition. It is about working with the currents that shape the world.

THE BASIC PHALLIC SPELL FORM

Start by choosing a representation of the phallus. This might be a wand, candle, carved charm, root, or even a drawn figure on parchment. Cleanse it with smoke or salt. Then anoint it with oil. Cinnamon for attraction. Dragon's blood for power. Patchouli for grounding. You are not just dressing an object—you are awakening it. Naming it. Giving it breath.

Next, carve your intention into its surface. Words, sigils, or names. Whisper to it. Speak desire, command, or prayer. Then set it upright—always upright—and place it where it can receive the energies you seek: in sunlight for vitality, moonlight for fertility, crossroads for movement, or the bedroom for passion.

Light a candle beside it. Offer herbs, coins, or drops of liquor. Treat it like an honored spirit. Leave it for one full cycle—sunrise to sunrise or moonrise to moonrise—then bury it, burn it, or carry it, depending on the nature of the spell.

SPELL FOR POWERFUL SPEECH AND COMMAND

Begin with a penis-shaped candle in red or black— colors of Mars and the throat chakra in balance. Carve into the wax your full name along with the words: "command," "clarity," and "conviction." Dress the candle with clove oil to sharpen your tongue and bay leaf oil to draw respect. Place a tiger's eye stone underneath the base to amplify inner confidence and guard against being silenced.

On your altar or work table, stand tall. Place the candle between your hands as if gripping a scepter. Speak this aloud with force:

"By rod and root, I claim my voice.
By fire and flame, I speak with choice.
Let no word falter, no will bend—
I cast, I claim, I command, I send."

As the candle burns, read aloud a list of things you need to say or express—truths, confrontations, boundaries, or goals. Let the wax melt completely.

Once cooled, wrap the remains in red flannel and keep in your bag, pocket, or on your desk when you must speak boldly.

SPELL TO DRAW IN A LOVER

Select a red or pink phallic candle—smooth and curved like a beckoning finger. Dress it with rose oil, a few drops of honey, and your personal essence if you're comfortable (saliva, bath water, or a tear). Surround the base with dried damiana, rose petals, and a lock of your hair or a photo. Write your desire on parchment: be specific, but leave room for magic to choose the best match.

Each night for seven nights, light the candle and say:

"Rise with heat, rise with grace,
Call the one who shares my space.
Lover, friend, now find your way—
By flame and flesh, come here and stay."

On the final night, take all the remaining wax, parchment, and herbs and bury them near your front step, beneath a flowering bush, or in a potted plant by your bed. This seals the invitation with rooted energy.

SPELL FOR PROTECTION USING THE PHALLUS

Use a carved phallic charm such as a fascinum or palad khik—metal, clay, or wood. If possible, choose one that feels heavy in your hand. Anoint it with saltwater for purity or a protective oil like hyssop, frankincense, or cast-off evil. Whisper into it:

"Stand before me, iron rod,
Break their curse and bless this sod.
Erect, unshaken, bold and bright,
Ward me with your ancient might."

Hang the charm above your door, near your bed, or tuck it in a red or black flannel pouch and carry it. Recharge it once a month by holding it in flame-light and breathing across it three times. This keeps it alert and watchful.

EMBODIED PHALLIC WORK

The body itself—when approached as sacred—becomes the first altar. For those who carry a penis, it can be awakened as a living wand, a vessel of energy and will. This is not vulgarity. It is ancient practice. Begin by cleansing yourself—bathe with herbs like rosemary and basil, then sit or stand in stillness. With intention and consent, touch or hold the phallus as if it were a candle made of flesh and breath.

Breathe slowly and visualize a golden light rising from your root to your crown. Speak:

"This is the wand that breathes and burns,
The axis of will, where power turns.
I charge this form to cast and send,
To call, to bless, to break, to bend."

Use this embodied wand in solo work, in partnership, or even by simply directing energy into objects like charged talismans, candles, or written spells. Release or climax is not required—only will and focus. If you do choose to release, let it be on purpose. Let it be part of the spell.

For those without a physical phallus, the energy still lives in you. Visualize it rising from the sacral or solar plexus chakra—shimmering, reaching. Use a wand or your finger as a conduit. Speak the same words. The rod of power is not limited by flesh. It belongs to the spirit.

SPELL TO PREVENT INFIDELITY (HISTORIC CURSE BINDING)

This is a spell with teeth—meant for when betrayal has been proven and hearts are on the line. Shape a wax figure to represent the unfaithful partner, ideally from black or brown wax. Into the figure, insert three pins: one through the feet to halt straying, one through the heart to bind affection, and one directly through the phallus to deaden desire outside the home.

As you work, say:

"By iron sharp and waxen form,
I bind your lust, your straying storm.
No seed to spill, no path to stray,
Your root is fixed, and there shall stay."

Wrap the doll in black cloth and drip red sealing wax over the bundle. Bury it at a crossroads if you want justice, or beneath a heavy stone if you wish to suppress the behavior without stirring further trouble. This is old magic, and not to be used lightly. But it is effective.

SPELL TO ATTRACT MALE FERTILITY

Fertility is the meeting of seed and soil, timing and trust. To bless a man with fruitful energy, take a red candle and carve into it a series of phallic sigils or fertility symbols—upward arrows, spirals, seeds, and sunbursts. Place it in a flowerpot filled with fresh soil. Around it, arrange basil for virility, rosemary for health, and a hardboiled egg as a living charm of potential.

Light the candle and chant:

"Let the rod rise with fertile might,
Seed and soil, day and night.
From root to leaf, from stem to crown,
Bless the loins where life is found."

Let the candle burn while meditating on abundance, health, and strong lineage. When the candle is spent, bury the egg and leftover wax in a sunny spot—preferably near a tree or garden. The energy you've planted will grow over time.

SPELL FOR MASCULINE CONFIDENCE

Confidence is not just a mindset—it's a spell you wear like armor. Take a wooden wand or charm and paint it gold. If you don't have gold paint, wrap the charm in gold thread. Anoint it with bay leaf oil, frankincense, or crushed fennel. This is your token of flame and backbone.

Lie down or sit comfortably. Place the charm on your solar plexus and breathe deeply. As you exhale, say:

"I rise, I stand, I move with flame,
No fear shall halt, no doubt shall claim.
By rod and will, I carve my place,
With lifted head and steady pace."

Let the charm absorb your breath, your voice, your intention. Carry it daily—in a pocket, a necklace, or pinned inside your clothes. Recharge under the sun, or by whispering affirmations into it during your morning ritual.

SPELL FOR SACRED UNION (SEX MAGIC RITE)

This is a rite of union—of body and spirit, wand and chalice. Prepare two candles: one shaped as a phallus, the other as a cup, chalice, or yoni. Dress both in amber oil to warm the senses and attract loving spirits. Place them facing each other on your altar with a small mirror behind them, reflecting their union into the spiritual realm.

Light both candles and say:

"By flame and flesh, by wand and cup,
Let our bodies rise and spirits sup.
Union holy, union bright,
We merge as one in love and light."

If working with a partner, hold hands. If working solo, place your hands over your heart and pelvis. Let the breath synchronize with desire. This is a spell of joining—not only with another person, but with your own wholeness. Once the candles burn halfway, snuff them gently. Relight them only when you wish to rekindle this connection.

Curse Reversal Using Phallic Force

When another has cursed you—twisted your name or knotted your road—this spell turns their venom back upon them. Begin with a red phallic candle. Carve it with reversal symbols such as backward spirals, mirror runes, or your name written in reverse. Drive a black iron nail through the candle's middle. Dress it with a mix of cayenne pepper, sulfur, and salt.

Speak:

"I break your bind, I twist your thread,
I raise the rod—your curse is dead.
Back to sender, sharp and swift,
My wand defends with sacred gift."

Light the candle. Watch until the nail falls free—this is your sign that the reversal is complete. Collect the wax and bury it in graveyard dirt, compost, or near a thorn bush. The phallus has done its work—bold, upright, and fiercely protective.

SPELL TO REIGNITE SEXUAL PASSION

When the flame grows dim but the ember still burns, this spell calls the fire back to life. Take a carved phallic charm—wood, resin, or wax. Wrap it in red cloth with cinnamon bark, orange peel, and a sliver of dried ginger. Whisper your partner's name as you tie the bundle shut.

Say:

"By flame unquenched and root unshorn,
Let heat and hunger be reborn.
Touch, and taste, and spark renew,
Old fire rise in something new."

Place the bundle beneath the bed, tucked discreetly or sewn into the underside of a pillow. Every third night, unwrap and re-anoint it with oil of cinnamon or musk. If you have pets that might disturb it, you may choose to place it under the mattress to keep it safe from snooping dogs or cats. The charm becomes a hearth—warming and ready.

PHALLUS OF THE PATH OPENER

When doors won't budge and roads won't clear, the rod of opening clears the way. Place a phallic figure—metal, wood, or clay—on a dish filled with road dust, tobacco, and a few drops of High John the Conqueror oil. Light a white candle beside it and say:

"Wand of roads, of choice, of fate,
Open doors and guide the gate.
No block shall stand, no fear remain,
With this rod, I rise again."

Sit with the figure and candle for at least ten minutes, visualizing your path unfolding like a ribbon. Afterward, carry a pinch of the dirt in a sachet or your shoe for seven days. Recharge weekly until the road opens or the spell fulfills.

JUSTICE SPELL AGAINST ABUSERS

Some wounds demand reckoning. To call forth justice against those who misuse power—especially sexual power—this spell acts as both curse and consequence. Using a root or candle shaped like a phallus, bind it with red thread to a poppet or image of the offender. Pierce it with thorns, sewing needles, or bent nails.

Speak:

"You used the rod to wound, not bless,
So now your strength I shall suppress.
By thorn and fire, pain shall be,
Until your harm no longer breathes."

Burn the thread and any tags or names. Dispose of the remains in running water or throw them across your left shoulder at a crossroads without looking back. This is not a light working. Cleanse thoroughly after. Justice walks with a sharp staff.

SPELL TO EMPOWER QUEER DESIRE

Magic should always include those on the edges, those with sacred fire in their step. To bless and empower queer desire, anoint a phallic charm with ylang-ylang, lavender, and orange blossom oil. Wrap it in a rainbow cloth or one dyed with colors meaningful to you.

Say:

"This rod is mine, this power mine,
By choice, by fire, by sacred sign.
Love that dares and love that stands,
Unashamed in heart and hands."

Place it on your altar or wear it discreetly. It's not about seeking acceptance—it's about standing in full power. The phallus is not only straight and narrow. It curves, it dances, it transforms.

SPELL TO CLAIM AUTHORITY IN A NEW SPACE

When you move into a new space—home, workplace, temple—it's vital to declare your energetic presence. Tap a wand or phallic charm on the ground at each corner of the space. As you do, sprinkle black salt or tobacco and say:

"With rod in hand, I stake this land,
No harm shall cross, no foe shall stand.
My will, my word, my sacred claim,
I mark this space in my own name."

Repeat monthly or after any spiritual cleansing. This spell establishes you as the energetic sovereign of the space.

DREAM SPELL OF THE WANDERING PHALLUS

Phallic energy doesn't sleep. It dreams, wanders, and brings messages. On the night of the full moon, anoint a small phallic charm with mugwort oil. Place it under your pillow and say:

"Show me truths in secret night,
Wand of sleep, reveal with light.
Where the rod shall point or roam,
Guide my soul back safely home."

Keep a journal beside the bed. Write down every dream, no matter how strange or erotic. Over time, patterns will emerge and the spirit of the rod will speak through symbols.

SPELL FOR ARTISTIC INSPIRATION

Art is born from fire. To stoke the creative wand, place a small phallic charm in a jar filled with rosemary, lemon zest, pencil shavings, and a pinch of sugar. Light a yellow candle beside it and say:

"Wand of words, and hand of flame,
Let vision rise and find its name.
From thought to stroke, from spark to ink,
Let nothing stall the will I think."

Place the jar on your desk or workspace. Shake it before writing, painting, singing, or crafting. The charm acts as a fuse, lighting the fire each time you sit down to create.

SPELL TO BREAK SHAME AROUND SEXUALITY

Shame is a binding that dulls the wand. To break it, take a phallic figure and anoint it with myrrh and patchouli. Carve your name or initials onto its base. In private, place it before a mirror and speak:

"I cast off shame, I shed old skin,
The sacred rod now wakes within.
No fear, no guilt, no whispered lie—
This power's mine and I know why."

Wrap it in red silk and store it under your bed or on your altar. Revisit the charm when doubt creeps in. The phallus remembers your truth.

SPELL FOR SACRED SELF-PLEASURE

This spell is for solo work—but it is not small magic. To sanctify your sexual energy, prepare a bath with rose petals, cinnamon sticks, and a few drops of sandalwood oil. Light a red candle and place a phallic charm nearby. As you bathe, say:

"This body's mine, this fire too,
And all I feel is strong and true.
No shame, no fear, just sacred flame,
I pleasure self and call my name."

You may choose to climax or not. What matters is intention. This rite rewrites old scripts and calls your power back into your body.

SPELL OF THE SOLAR ROD (SUNLIGHT EMPOWERMENT)

For those who feel drained or directionless, the phallus can be charged with solar fire. At noon, place a phallic charm in a dish of salt and citrine. Set it outside in full sun and say:

"O rod of gold, of shining crown,
Burn away what pulls me down.
Light the path and firm my tread,
From solar fire, I rise and shed."

After three hours, bring the charm inside. Carry it when strength or clarity is needed. This is a spell of revival, not aggression. The rod becomes a torch.

CLOSING THE WORK

Always ground after spellwork. Eat something. Touch the earth. Wiggle your bare toes in the grass. Or just rest. And if you have performed baneful work, always spiritually cleanse yourself. Thank the spirit of the phallus, whether embodied or symbolic. Wrap the tool, store it with herbs, or dispose of the remains with   care.

The phallus, when honored, becomes more than symbol. It becomes spell. Direction. Power. It becomes the thing that cuts through illusion, that blesses the body, that opens the way. It is yours to wield.

RECLAIMING THE SACRED MASCULINE

The phallus has traveled a long and winding road—rising, falling, worshiped, hidden, carved into stone, buried under shame, raised again in defiance, and whispered back into power. It has been called sacred, obscene, divine, profane, magical, and dangerous. But through every turn, one thing remains: it endures.

And now, it returns—not as a joke, not as a weapon, not as a banner for control—but as a key. A living, directional key. A symbol of sacred will ready to be held by those who understand what it truly is.

To reclaim the phallus is not to glorify masculinity. It is to untangle it. To remember what it was before the wounds of war, before the shadow of patriarchy, before domination replaced direction and arrogance replaced authority. The phallus was never meant to dominate. It was meant to channel. To protect. To bless. It was a signpost. A staff. A wand of sacred fire.

In every tradition we've studied—from Egypt to Bhutan, from Rome to the rural roads of Appalachia—the phallus stood for more than anatomy. It stood for the ability to move the world with intention. To carve a path, to bless a field, to summon healing, to hold power with clarity and care. It marked the boundary between life and death, the doorway between flesh and spirit, the upright line between above and below.

When we say "sacred masculine," we are not talking about men. We are talking about current. The phallus, as magical tool, has always belonged to the one who can carry it with responsibility. It does not require testicles. It requires integrity. It does not demand a deep voice. It demands clear direction. The sacred masculine is the energy that chooses. That acts. That moves. That pierces through confusion and says: this is the way.

That's what this book has always been about—not just recovering a symbol, but remembering a truth. One that our ancestors knew before doctrine took the reins. Before symbols were censored or stripped of their meaning. They knew that the phallus was a spiritual technology. It called down rain. It kept out evil. It sparked crops to rise and lovers to return. They knew that when you raised the rod in ritual, you weren't just working with flesh—you were working with flame.

So what does reclamation look like?

It starts with ritual. With speaking the word aloud, without flinching. With dressing the candle, fixing the charm, anointing the wand, and naming what it is. It's standing at your altar, candle lit, rod in hand, and saying: this is not a toy. This is a tool. This is the force that directs my will. It blesses where I tell it to bless. It binds where I tell it to bind. It protects where I say the line is drawn.

Reclamation looks like choosing not to whisper. Not to water it down. Not to let the phallus be reduced to ridicule or feared into silence. It means lifting it up again—not to dominate, but to hold sacred. To remember that the rod was never just flesh. It was the flame at the center of the body. The signal fire between soul and earth.

For those who work magic in queer bodies, in femme bodies, in trans bodies, in wounded bodies—this reclamation is especially vital. Because power has long been gatekept by those who didn't deserve it. The sacred masculine doesn't belong to them. It belongs to the ones who can carry it with clean hands and strong hearts. It belongs to you.

To reclaim the phallus is not to reach for conquest. It is to reach for alignment. It is to say: I will no longer be ashamed of the power that moves through me. I will use it to heal. To love. To command. To build. To protect what's holy and cast out what's not. I will lift the wand not in arrogance, but in purpose. And when I do, I will not flinch.

Because the phallus was never the problem. The misuse of it was.

What happens when we reclaim the sacred masculine? We open the door to a magic that moves cleanly— like lightning that strikes but does not burn, like the sun that feeds but does not blind. We allow masculine energy to serve again, not as master, but as protector, partner, and guide. And in doing so, we restore the balance that has always been missing.

That's the work. Not to conjure a new power from thin air, but to remember the one that's already lived in our bones for generations. Not to lift one kind of magic above another, but to restore what's been missing—to return the key to the altar where it belongs. And not to copy what's been done poorly in the past, but to rise above it. To do it better. With clarity. With fire. And with soul.

When you hold the rod—whatever it represents in your practice—claim it. Speak its name. Use it with purpose. Not to show off. Not to dominate. Not to reenact the old wounds of power. Use it as it was meant to be used: in motion, in memory, in mastery. Let your work be a reflection of deeper understanding, not borrowed power.

Bless what was once feared. Reclaim what was once silenced. Let your entire practice become a living spell—one that speaks not just to the spirits, but to the world around you.

Because when the phallus is held with reverence, it becomes what it was always meant to be: a tool that moves energy forward. And for those willing to raise it with purpose, it still works. Always has.

CONCLUSION

The phallus isn't just flesh. It never was. It's form, force, direction—the upright flame, the carved wand, the root buried deep in the dark that still pushes up toward light. It's the motion inside every spell that dares to say, *"I will."* In every culture, in every era, there have been those who knew how to use that motion. Not to dominate. But to make things happen.

You'll find the phallus everywhere people have tried to name what moves us and what makes things real. In temples. In myths. In spells written by candlelight. In carved stone, polished wood, dripping wax. In the corners of altars and the heat of a dream. It doesn't belong to one gender. It doesn't belong to one path. It belongs to the current of will—wherever it rises, whoever carries it with clarity.

We've seen the phallus misused. We've seen it mocked, weaponized, turned into spectacle or shame. We've seen it reduced to a punchline in one breath, then glorified as a symbol of power in the next— usually by those who neither earned nor understood its weight. But none of that ever touched the real current underneath. Because power doesn't vanish just because people forget how to respect it. The rod still works. And for those who carry it with reverence, it's always been more than a shape. It's a signal. A tool of direction and motion. A key that unlocks the next step forward.

This has never been about worship. It's about remembering. Remembering what the phallus was *before* it was politicized. Before the sacred masculine was twisted into control, stripped of care, and mistaken for dominance. The true phallic current isn't about aggression—it's about intention. It's the part of the human spirit that chooses, that acts, that cuts through confusion and says, "This way." That energy isn't gendered. It's alive. It's sacred. And it belongs to anyone strong enough to hold it with purpose.

To work with the phallus is to make a choice. A choice to name what you want, to set energy in motion, and to do it cleanly. That might mean lighting a red candle dressed in oil and carved with a lover's name. It might mean planting a charm beneath your altar or raising a wand at a threshold and speaking your will into the world. And it might mean holding your own body like a tool of fire and breath, not out of ego—but out of awareness. Out of truth. Out of spell.

Because the phallus isn't sacred because of what it looks like. It's sacred because of what it *does*. It draws down fire. It clears the path. It blesses beds and marks territory and opens doors that don't respond to words alone. It's a symbol of divine willingness. The willingness to rise. To act. To lead. To protect what matters. To claim a space with your presence and shape it with your will.

When you hold that symbol—whether in your hand, on your altar, or in your spirit—you are stepping into a legacy that reaches back through stone and fire and prayer. A legacy of farmers and warriors, witches and queens, conjurers and lovers. People who knew that the phallus wasn't a toy. It was technology. Spiritual, emotional, magical technology. And like all tools, its value depends on how it's used—and who dares to hold it with care.

Papa Coll

BIBLIOGRAPHY

Andrews, Tamra Lucid. *Symbol and Archetype in Human Sexuality.* University of Missouri Press. 2006.

Becker, Carl L. *Sacred Phallus: A Study of the Fertility Symbol in Ritual and Religion.* Inner Traditions. 1994.

Berger, Helen A. *A Community of Witches: Contemporary Neo-Paganism and Witchcraft in the United States.* University of South Carolina Press. 1999.

Bosch, Lynette. *Art, Liturgy, and Legend in Renaissance Toledo: The Mendoza and the Iglesia Primada.* Penn State University Press. 2000.

Bramly, Serge. *The Body: A New History of Western Representation.* Thames & Hudson. 2006.

Conner, Randy P., Sparks, David Hatfield & Sparks, Mariya. *Queering Creole Spiritual Traditions: Lesbian, Gay, Bisexual, and Transgender Participation in African-Inspired Traditions in the Americas.* Routledge. 2004.

Detienne, Marcel. *The Gardens of Adonis: Spices in Greek Mythology.* Princeton University Press. 1989.

Frazer, James George. *The Golden Bough: A Study in Magic and Religion.* Macmillan. 1922.

Jennings, Hargrave. *Phallic Worship.* Kessinger Publishing. 2003. (Originally published 1874.)

Leick, Gwendolyn. *Sex and Eroticism in Mesopotamian Literature.* Routledge. 1994.

Neumann, Erich. *The Origins and History of Consciousness.* Princeton University Press. 1954.

Ogden, Daniel. *Magic, Witchcraft, and Ghosts in the Greek and Roman Worlds: A Sourcebook.* Oxford University Press. 2002.

Yronwode, Catherine & White, Gregory Lee. *Amulets, Charms, and Talismans in the Hoodoo and Conjure Tradition.* Lucky Mojo Curio Company. 2021.